AMERICAN INDIAN BEADWORK

J. F. "Buck" Burshears, a longtime Boy Scout leader, formed within the Scouts a unique group known as the Koshare Indian Dancers. The boys interpreted native dances, made costumes, and studied the history and lives of various tribes. During his travels with the Koshares, Mr. Burshears amassed one of the most extensive collections of Indian artifacts and handicrafts in the country.

"Buck" Burshears

W. Ben Hunt traveled widely, visiting pueblos and hogans of the Southwest and reservations of the Midwest and Canada to acquaint himself with Indian lore. While he was living and camping with the Indians, they gave him the name "Tasunka Witko," which means Crazy Horse. He was also known as "Kachina Ben" because of the Kachina Indian dolls he was so adept at carving. In addition to being a well-known Boy Scout leader and adviser, Mr. Hunt was a writer who regularly contributed to professional and scouting magazine articles on Indian and other handicraft projects.

Ben Hunt

American Indian
BEADWORK

By

W. *BEN* *HUNT*

and

J. F. "BUCK" BURSHEARS

COLLIER BOOKS
Macmillan Publishing Company
NEW YORK

COLLIER MACMILLAN PUBLISHERS
LONDON

Macmillan Publishing Company
866 Third Avenue, New York, N.Y. 10022
Collier Macmillan Canada, Inc.

Library of Congress Catalog Card Number: 75-185636

ISBN 0-02-011700-0

FIRST COLLIER BOOKS EDITION 1971

29 28 27 26 25 24 23

Macmillan books are available at special discounts for
bulk purchases for sales promotions, premiums, fund-
raising, or educational use. For details, contact:

Special Sales Director
Macmillan Publishing Company
866 Third Avenue
New York, N.Y. 10022

Printed in the United States of America

FOREWORD

"I want to make an Indian beaded belt!" a young boy demanded of his handicraft instructor in camp. Such demands are made every day in thousands of camps and craftshops. To fulfill the many requests for craft instruction, especially on how to make a beaded belt and other beaded costumes of the American Indian, this book has been written.

The romance and beauty of the costumes of the American Indian have so endeared them to children and adults alike all over the world, that it is natural for every child to want to make something Indian. Often attempts are very feeble, for the uninitiated cannot grasp the method artistry of design, and his work usually ends up in a miserable failure, both in construction and design. A beginner often makes a few diamonds and triangles, and finishes by putting his initials on a few of the other symmetrical designs. If he does finish these first pieces in this manner, he is sure to realize very soon that it is not Indian.

This book has been published not as an exhaustive study of design and methods, but as a handicraft guide for those seeking the fundamentals of construction and ideas of design. Experienced students of Indian lore often create creditable designs, but not until they have made a complete study of it, for our Anglo minds seldom function like that of the Indian.

It is hoped that this book will be accepted as favorably as Ben Hunt's other books on allied Indian crafts.

ACKNOWLEDGMENTS

To Delmar and Stanley Kimball, Koshare Chiefs, whose artistry and painstaking labor graphed the designs as they were collected by J. F. Burshears.

To Lester Griswold for his inspiration and loan of graphing cuts which were used for the designs.

To Ralph Hubbard, great teacher and authority, for inspiration directly and indirectly which started the Koshare Indian Dancers.

To Chester Denton for photographing the costume collection.

DEDICATION

This book is respectfully dedicated to the
Koshare Indian Dancers, Boy Scouts of Troop
230, La Junta, Colorado.

Their enthusiasm and interest in their craft-
work gave the authors the idea that a book such
as this would be helpful to all those who
wanted to learn and practice the beadwork
arts of the American Indian.

CONTENTS

SECTION 1

SHORT HISTORY OF BEADWORK OF THE AMERICAN INDIAN

Beads of various types have been used for ornamentation by man since the beginning of time. These have taken many forms, such as seeds, shells, claws, bones, and stones.

The beads used by the American Indian at the time of Columbus' discovery were no different than those of other primitive people. Belts, woven of wampum or shell, were common among many tribes who had access to shells. With the discovery of America and the coming of settlers, traders soon found their stocks of glass beads readily accepted as trade for furs. The fur traders prospered, and soon trading expeditions went deeper and deeper into the woods and plains country. Before the advent of the European seed bead, most plains and woodland Indians used porcupine quills dyed in various colors for decoration of their better clothes. With the coming of beads they replaced the quills or combined the beads with the quillwork. The geometrical designs to which quills lent themselves were the most generally followed. With the coming of the missionaries with their floral embroidered vestments, the Lake Indians and, more recently, others applied their beads to such flowered designs.

Many tribal characteristics of design are recognizable. The designs of the Lake Indians, for example, were more often flowered; those of the Sioux or plains Indian were geometrical, and the Blackfoot and northern plains Indian had more massive geometrical designs. Many tribes applied animal pictures to vests and bandoleers. For pure beauty of geometrical design, few, if any, excelled the Apache. Their close cousin, the Navajo, expressed similar artistry in rugs.

The following pages are made up of various designs collected from many parts of the United States. Many of them are from the private collection of J. F. Burshears, others come from the Smithsonian Institute, Washington, D. C., the Field Museum, Chicago, Ill., and the Jefferson Memorial at St. Louis, Mo., and pieces collected by the Koshare Indian Dancers of La Junta, Colo. Many thousands of designs are available. These are relatively few, but they give a cross section of the arts of different tribes. Similar designs are found in many sections due to the fact that the Indians were great traders. It is common to find Indians thousands of miles away wearing a Chippewa breechcloth and belt of floral designs, or the Pueblos of New Mexico wearing beaded costumes of the northern tribes.

The Pueblos and Navajos did very little beadwork, and it has been only recently that Santa Clara squaws have been making belts, following geometrical designs. They may have learned this art in the schools or picked it up during their travels.

A beautiful bag, that came from a Two Gray Hills trading post on the Navajo Reservation, shows that the beadworker had applied the design of a fine Navajo rug. Some of the Utes have created purses and belts of realistic floral designs. The Lake Indians also have created some realistic floral designs, but many are only abstractions of floral designs.

Some fine beadwork is still in the possession of present-day Indians who have not lost the art and are still making beautiful pieces. Most of the fine pieces have been collected by museums or collectors, and original owners have been forced to dispose of their priceless pieces at a fraction of their value in order to be able to exist.

USING BEAD DESIGNS

It has been the authors' experience that young people, especially, when confronted by designs as shown in this book, have a tendency to choose an elaborate and intricate piece of beading with which to begin. After several attempts at weaving, they invariably look at their first attempt and decide to discard or rip it and do it over again, or they try to sell or trade it off to someone who is too lazy to do beading. Therefore, it is much more sensible to have them begin with, let us say, a narrow, nine- or eleven-bead-wide belt or headband with a repeat design. That will give them the *feel* of beading.

Many elaborate designs are shown in the following pages, but there is no hodgepodge or mixture of design. Each section or unit illustrated is, as a rule, a design that can be repeated in one strip. There are times when two or more designs are incorporated on one strip but only when they match and do not clash.

A fine line is drawn between unity and monotony. For instance, when leg bands, shirtbands, and belt are all of the same design and color, it becomes monotonous, but when they are properly matched in color with pleasing variations, they will be uniform. When leg bands and shirtbands of entirely different design and color are used together, it usually is due to the fact that the owner bought or traded a set of strips and used them on one garment without thought. Or, perhaps he liked them well enough to overlook this difference. Everyone's taste differs, but it still is not advisable to crowd every design in one strip. A good design repeated is better than several unrelated designs and it will not be considered monotonous.

The designs in this book were drawn on graph paper and seem to be only for loom work. Graph paper was used to facilitate drawing as it would have been an endless task to draw all the beads individually, which had to

be done in drawing the rosette designs. For this work, graph paper could not be used. All designs drawn on graph paper can be used for any or all methods of beading described herein.

Making colored drawings in detail for floral beading also would be an endless undertaking and quite useless, as the placing of the beads is different in almost every instance and a drawing could not be followed. A slight change in the shape of a design would throw the whole scheme out of order as far as following it *to the bead,* as in squared designs. Therefore, many photographs of floral and figured beadwork have been included in the book. When the method described is followed, these designs can be easily drawn on material and, by following the general scheme of placing the lines of beads, can be executed without any difficulty. In floral appliquéd beading, no two persons work alike. Some sewed or appliquéd beadwork will be found to be of mill-run beads, while on other pieces the beads will be selected with the same meticulous care and patience used in fine loom work.

Quite often the beader will choose a design that is too narrow or too wide for the purpose which it is to serve. To make a wider strip, usually all that is necessary is to add more background beads to the outer sides. To enlarge a design or unit of design means that it will have to be enlarged in both directions, height and width, as beads are not flexible. As a rule, it is better to choose a wider design. However, a design can be beaded larger by adding as many beads to the width (of the design) as are needed. The Ogallala shirt strips on page 37 are good examples of the same design used in different widths. The originals had white backgrounds. The reason for the change in color is told at the end of this chapter.

To make a design narrower is more difficult,

as for instance in belt beading. By taking out two rows of beads, as a general rule, the design is changed somewhat, but this becomes necessary because it is impossible to shrink beads.

When looking for a design for a pipe bag, for instance, any pleasing design that fits the space can be used regardless of where it has been taken from. It may be one element or unit taken from a belt or a leg band. A few additional motifs can be added to the top and bottom or the sides to fill it out. After studying Indian designs, it seems quite simple to make changes in such ·designs. For instance, quite a few of the belt and band designs in Plate 3, such as the third belt from the top, are adaptable to small bags. The triangles as well as the diamonds can be made larger; in fact, almost any of the designs worked out in diamonds and triangles can be easily made larger. Also,

by taking out a few beads, some of the designs can be made smaller without any noticeable difference in design.

Now, a few words regarding colors. While these designs are taken from actual Indian pieces of beadwork, the colors may not suit everyone's taste. It may be desired to change the background. Turquoise backgrounds often are used on buckskin, and show up very nicely. Sometimes, however, the color of beads shown may not be obtainable. It must be remembered, however, that the contrast in color, as a rule, makes designs pop out. Therefore, to change a background usually means that the other colors must be changed also. This has been illustrated in the Ogallala Sioux shirt strips, using a turquoise blue background which necessitated changing the blues, that appeared in the original, to reds and yellows.

LOOMS

Loom beading is by far the most popular present-day method in spite of the fact that sewed beadwork shows up the best on large surfaces. Loom beading also is easier for the beginner, but certain things should be remembered. The most important of these is that the beads should be *selected*. By this is meant that all beads should be of uniform size, both in diameter and width. Loom beadwork with mill-run beads looks very rough, and it is only after a little practice in it that the uneven work is overcome. When beads first are picked up on a beading needle, their irregularities are not too apparent. Often the beads look perfect, but when they are pushed up between the warp threads, any irregularities are seen immediately. One larger bead will tend to make a bulge on an outer edge. That is the time to remove it and replace it with a bead of the correct size. Sometimes it is not the width of the bead that spoils the row, but one with

too large a hole. Such a bead tends to push up or drop down, which also breaks the regularity of the work. In time, a poor bead will be detected before it is picked up. Speaking of picking up, this is the time to explain the several methods. Everyone has different methods, or rather, let us say, different likes and dislikes.

One method of working is to have a shallow dish for each color of bead used. Small saucers are best and, of course, they should be white.

Another method, when not too many colors are used, is to throw all beads in one plate. This is not advisable, however, when red and vermilion beads, or dark blue and black are used on the same piece, because the wrong colors are too easily picked up. This is the method this author prefers because it requires only one or, at the most, two plates of beads, and does away with a lot of reaching which is not so good when the thread becomes short.

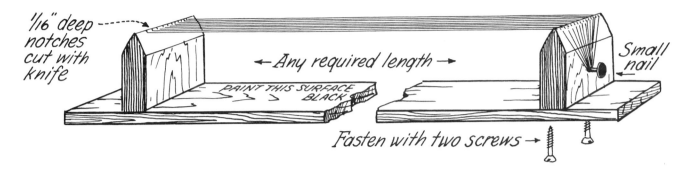

"1/16" deep notches cut with knife

← Any required length →

PAINT THIS SURFACE BLACK

Small nail

Fasten with two screws →

Fig. 1

Still another method, especially when beads are bought in strings, is to take a bead or beads off the string as they are needed and onto the needle. Each method has its good and bad points.

Now to continue with the looms. If the worker decides to buy a loom, that problem is easily settled. The drawback in bought looms is their short length. Even though the finished piece can be rolled up as it is being worked, it does not roll up too evenly, and the first part of it cannot be seen when it has been wound on the spool.

A loom long enough for the entire piece is preferable. Work and color can be compared, and the piece can be easily measured for length. Another good feature is that beading can be started in the middle and worked toward the two ends, thus making it easier to get the proper length. The loom shown in Figure 1 is easy to make and easy to work on. It can be adjusted as needed by simply taking out two screws and moving the one head. If the bottom board is dark or painted black, the beads will show up better while working.

Indians frequently use a boxlike loom made of thin wood strips. The warp threads are run all the way around in one continuous piece (Fig. 2). Notches seldom are cut for the individual threads as the beads govern the width regardless of how far apart the warp threads are.

A box loom must be made wide enough and the side pieces must be cut away so that the beader's knuckles will not be forever banging on the edges of the box. The side pieces should be of straight-grained, flexible wood, thin enough to be bent easily. When the work is ready to be shifted, the loom can be shortened by pressing the sides inward, thereby loosening the threads enough to do the shifting. Box looms were frequently used for wide weaving

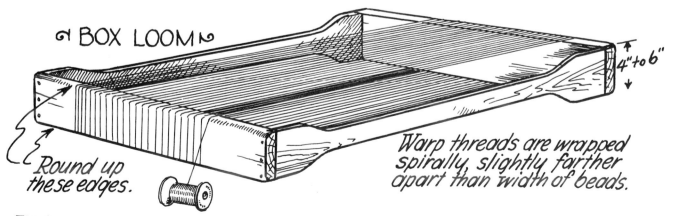

a BOX LOOM

4" to 6"

Round up these edges.

Warp threads are wrapped spirally, slightly farther apart than width of beads.

Fig. 2

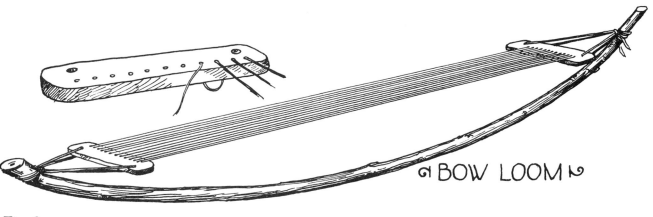

a BOW LOOM a

Fig. 3

for bandoleers, and for tobacco and other bags.

There is still another loom, more on the primitive side, made like the one shown in Figure 3. It consists of a wooden bow and two perforated pieces of wood or bone for spreaders. The bow is held between the knees while beading.

Thread for the warp should be strong, such as buttonhole thread, and preferably it should be waxed. That means it must be waxed after the loom has been strung. In making long strips of loom work, it is always a good policy to use *double threads* on the outer edges for added strength.

Beaded strips can be sewed to cloth backing strips, on a sewing machine, or they can be sewed on by hand. When using a sewing machine, the needle is guided between the outer row of beads and the second row. When sewing by hand the thread is caught around the outer double-warp threads.

When making a beaded belt, it is advisable to have the leather ½ inch wider than the bead strip or that the beaded strip is made ½ inch narrower than the belt to which it is to be sewed. The ¼ inch on either side will protect the outer threads from wear.

As belt leather usually is too thick to sew through, holes should be punched through the leather before attempting to sew. This can be done with an awl or by having a shoemaker

run his machine, with an unthreaded needle, along the line of sewing.

As a rule, when beading belts, an odd number of beads across are preferable. This gives you a center line of beads which usually is conducive to better design.

At the present time Indians find it rather difficult to obtain buckskin for backing such as they used in earlier years. However, there are other leathers through which a needle can be pushed rather easily. Therefore, when buying leather for beadwork, whether loom beading is to be sewed onto the leather or the separate beads are to be sewed directly onto it, a pierceable leather should be bought. When buying the leather, a needle should be taken along to try out the different leathers. Another thing to look for, when putting loom beadwork on leather, is that the leather does not stretch, as this puts a strain on the warp threads which in time breaks them. For soft leather belts, sewed beadwork is best.

Loom beading is done in the following manner. The loom is strung in width according to the number of beads desired. Then, for strength, it is good to wax the threads. Warp threads should be rather strong, for which a good nylon or buttonhole thread can be used. The weft or weaving thread should be as strong or rather as thick as can be threaded through the beads. The eye of a beading needle

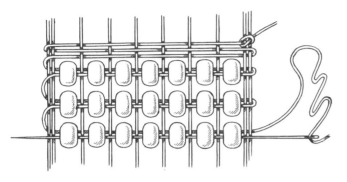

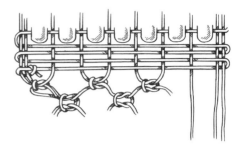

Fig. 5

Fig. 4

is of necessity very small so that also must be taken into consideration when selecting the thread. In other words, a thread that can be pushed through the eye of a regular beading needle will be the thread to use. It also should be remembered that the thread is doubled after it has gone through the eye of the needle, and that each thread goes through a bead twice; also that the hole in the bead is not too large. Therefore, if difficulty is encountered in getting a threaded needle through a bead the first time, it will be rather more difficult to get it through a second time, and the bead usually breaks in half. As a result, all beads must be removed to replace the broken one.

Now, with the needle threaded, weave with the weft thread, as shown in Figure 4, for about ¼ inch before the actual beading. After the first row of beads has been woven in place, pull the woven threads so they are rather tight, and knot over the edge warp threads on one side.

Please note that the beads are strung on the thread coming from the left side and under the warp for a right-handed person. Pick up the number of beads, of the desired color, on the needle, and try to get them uniform in size and shape. Slide the beads up on the thread to the left side and, while holding them taut with the right hand, push them up in place between the warp threads, with the first finger of the left hand. Hold them in that manner while the needle is passed through from the

right side and *over* the warp threads, as shown in Figure 4. Now you have one thread under and one thread over each warp thread, which keeps each bead in place. The weft thread also goes around each of the outer pair of warp threads. When the beading has been completed, weave across several times like you did at the beginning, and knot the thread (Fig. 5). Do not cut the end off short, but pass it back through several warp threads, knot it, and then cut it off. It is best to tie all knots inside the beading rather than over the outer warp threads, and keep all knots on the upper surface. Then, when finished, turn the work over so that the top becomes the bottom and consequently all the knots are hidden underneath.

After the work has been taken off the frame, the warp ends should be knotted together in twos and then in twos again, as shown in Figure 5. When sewing the strip onto the base, these ends are folded under before sewing down.

There is still another method of loom beading which is done with a heddle. This is more difficult insofar as the setup is concerned, and

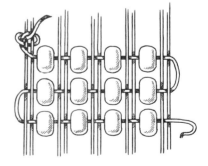

Fig. 6

only one thread goes through the bead while there are double-warp threads between the beads. Figure 6 shows how the beads are fastened or woven in, and anyone familiar with a regular weaving loom can easily see how it is done. This method is seldom used as there is only one thread through each bead. The type of loom required also is cumbersome.

It is advisable to discard all undesirable beads when fine loom beading is to be done. But, if the article will consist of sewed beadwork, such as rosettes, all beads not used should be saved. The reason for this will be shown and described later.

One thing that should be mentioned at this time is the base upon which beadwork later is sewed. Indians, when beading moccasin tops on soft buckskin, invariably sew a piece of cloth between the leather and the beads to prevent the threads from tearing when the leather stretches. It is good practice to under-lay all beadwork with good stout cloth such as felt or light canvas, for which strips and pieces from old felt hats or pennants can be used. Sometimes gummed package tape is pasted to the back of buckskin that is to be beaded. This will be further described later.

It also is well to have a small flat-nosed

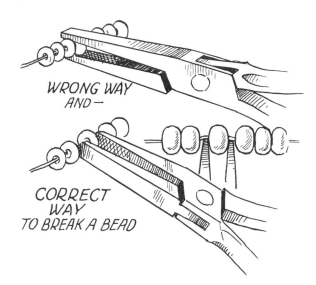

WRONG WAY
AND —

CORRECT WAY TO BREAK A BEAD

Fig. 7

pliers on hand for breaking beads. Quite frequently it will be found that there are too many beads on a thread. Oftentimes, by simply breaking a bead, it will not be unnecessary to unthread the needle and pull off the whole string of beads. There are, of course, many ways of breaking beads, but if it is done as shown in Figure 7, the thread will not be cut and it will prevent more trouble.

Another method of breaking beads is to push a large needle or small awl through the bead, which will crack the bead.

SEWED BEADWORK

Among the plains Indians, loom beadwork rarely is seen. Even for narrow strips, such as brow bands and arm bands, the beads were sewed directly to the cloth or buckskin, whichever was used. The plains Indians used more beadwork than the woodland Indians, and they used heavier buckskin or elkskin. Also, the skins the plains Indians tanned, as a rule, were not as soft as the smoke-tanned buckskin of the central woodland Indians, nor were they as thin.

The western Indians used sinew to sew on their beads, which is stiffer than thread and does not rot so easily. The sinew is moistened as each string of beads is sewed down. It pulls the beads tight and, on some of the Crow beadwork, it actually seems to be imbedded in the hide. The sinew-sewed beadwork, sewed on with the commonly called lazy-squaw stitch, lies in ridges, so to speak, and when a hand is passed over it, it feels rather solid. Lazy-squaw stitching sewed with thread does not feel that way, although it will have that appearance if done correctly.

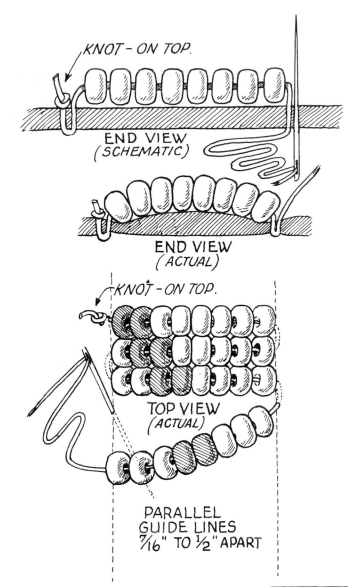

KNOT - ON TOP.

END VIEW
(SCHEMATIC)

END VIEW
(ACTUAL)

KNOT - ON TOP.

TOP VIEW
(ACTUAL)

PARALLEL
GUIDE LINES
7/16" TO 1/2" APART

Fig. 8

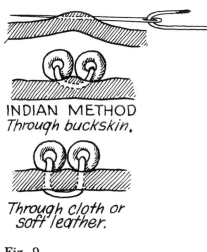

INDIAN METHOD
Through buckskin.

*Through cloth or
soft leather.*

Fig. 9

Lazy-squaw stitching is shown in Figures 8 and 9. The Indian, as a rule, does not sew through the entire thickness of the skin but only through half of it. But, when sewing with thread as the Crows do on moccasins and small work, they sew through the skin. The best method for our needs is to sew this stitch with waxed carpet thread, through the skin or cloth. The thread is knotted and brought up from below to begin; the beads are strung to the proper number or width, and the needle is thrust straight down alongside the last bead, then up again, the distance away to be in line for the next string (Fig. 8).

For beginners and where buckskin is not available, heavy cloth or canvas or pennant felt should be used for a base. That, in turn, is sewed onto the garment. In sewing with the lazy-squaw stitch on buckskin, no base is needed, as the pull of the hide will not be so direct on the short threads as it would be on loom beading with its long-warp threads. In sewing on felt or cloth for breechcloths, legging or shirt strips, or pipe and bandoleer bags, a backing of good light canvas is advisable to prevent stretching.

The designs should be drawn on the material in some fashion. When sewing machines are handy, the following method can be used. Draw

Fig. 10

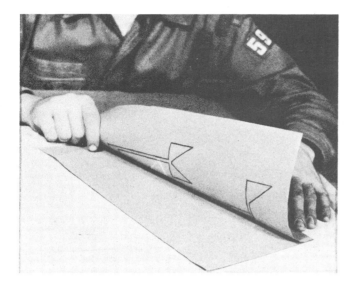

Fig. 11

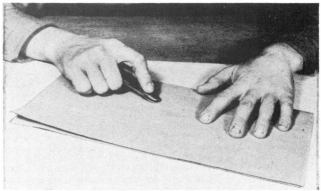

Fig. 12

out the design, let us say for a breechcloth, on a sheet of plain paper, such as craft paper. If the design is symmetrical, one half can be drawn first with a soft pencil as shown in Figure 10. The paper then is folded through the center with the drawn design on the inside, and is rubbed with a smooth surface over the design until the half design is transferred to the other half of the inside of the folded paper, as shown in Figures 11 and 12. If the transferred lines are not clear enough, they should be gone over with a pencil as shown in Figure 13.

Another way of transferring the second half of a symmetrical design is as shown in Figure 14. One half of the design is drawn with a pencil and the paper is folded down the center. A sheet of carbon paper then is placed on the table, face up, and the folded paper is laid upon it. Then, by going over the pencil lines with a hard pencil or a stylus, the design is transferred to the other half of the sheet, thus forming a complete pattern.

The paper then is basted onto the back of the cloth. With the sewing machine, the outline of the design should be sewed with white thread on dark cloth, and vice versa. The paper can be left on the back, but the sewing will show nicely on the right side to be followed with the beadwork. In lazy-squaw beading, most of the beading will be in the form of parallel lines, between which the rows of beads are sewed. These parallel guide

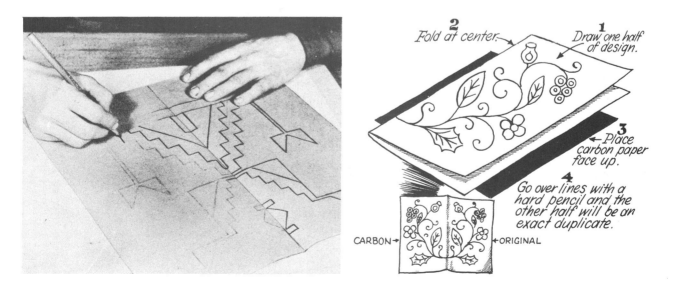

Fig. 13

Fig. 14

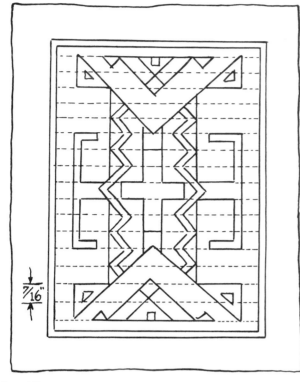

Fig. 15

7/16"

or colored pencil. Working on black velveteen, the author very successfully used white water color and a fine brush to lay out the design in a thin line. From 6 to 8 beads on a cross thread are the easiest to handle. Eight beads usually fill in nicely between lines 7/16 inch apart.

When sewing beads to cloth, regardless of the stitch used, the cloth should be tacked to some sort of frame. It is nice working on a frame that is clamped to the edge of a table, but some may prefer holding the frame in their lap. Whichever method is chosen and regardless of how the work is held, the cloth should be put on a frame, especially for large areas. Bands also can be worked easier if the ends are fastened to keep the band taut. Thumb tacks can be used to tack the work to the frame. The frame can be made of thin crate lumber, ¼ by 1½ inches, simply nailed at the corners.

Frames for belts and strips can be made as shown in Figure 16.

To make rosettes, the material can be placed in a pair of embroidery hoops.

Another commonly used method of beading is called appliquéd work, because a string of

lines also can be sewed into the design, but usually they can be drawn in with black or colored pencil, as shown in Figure 15.

On some materials the design outlines can be drawn with a ball-point pen, or with a black

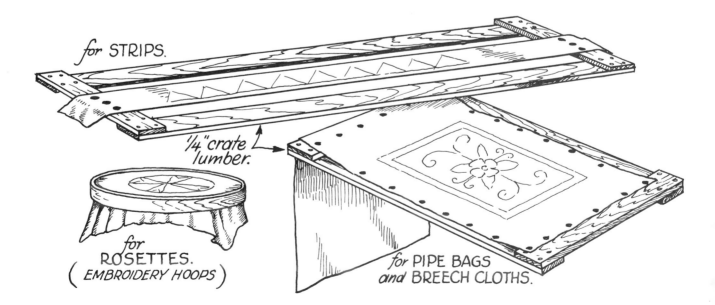

for STRIPS.

¼" crate lumber.

for ROSETTES.
(EMBROIDERY HOOPS)

for PIPE BAGS
and BREECH CLOTHS.

Fig. 16

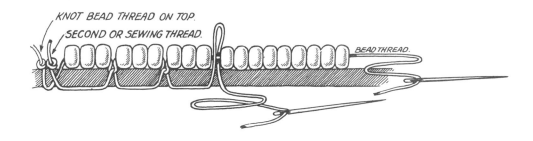

Fig. 17

beads is appliquéd or sewed to the cloth. This method is used by both plains and woodland Indians for floral designs.

The design is put on the cloth in one of the manners previously described, and the cloth is tacked to a frame. The thread is fastened on top, and the beads are strung on one thread and sewed down onto the cloth with another needle and thread, as shown in Figure 17. It is most advisable to use as heavy a piece of thread as the beads will permit.

A word here regarding knots would not be amiss. While it would seem that the proper thing to do would be to tie knots on the back of the material, tying them on the face is a much better practice. It is easier to make the knots, they can be more readily covered by the beading, and last but not least, these knots will not be worn off as quickly as they would be if they were on the back of the material.

ROSETTES

A good practice job for appliqué work is to make a pair of rosettes for a headband. Beads that had been discarded can be used for this purpose. Before beginning, it would be a good idea to study the color charts of rosettes. Here and there, narrow and wider beads are used to cut down or fill in space, for which odd-sized beads come in handy. Old felt-hat brims are excellent bases for rosettes.

Begin in the center with one bead and then string four or six beads for the first row. These may not fit so well, but the best that can be done will be satisfactory. The second thread, which is now knotted and brought up through the felt, is used to sew down this first row of beads. Three or four stitches may be necessary. For the next row, the beads should be threaded on the bead thread, and should be *fitted* around the first row, using whichever color has been selected. When the beads have been properly threaded so they fit nicely, they should be sewed on with the second needle

and thread, as close to the other row as possible, without forcing them. This procedure should be continued until a rosette has been completed. When each circle of beads has been

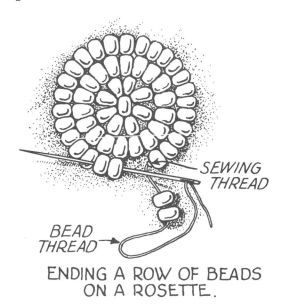

SEWING THREAD

BEAD THREAD

ENDING A ROW OF BEADS ON A ROSETTE.

Fig. 18

completed, the thread should be sewed through the first one or two beads again to pull the ends together without leaving a gap, as shown in Figure 18. By the time a rosette has been completed, it will have been learned that there is a great difference in beads. If the threads have not been pulled too tight, the rosette should be perfectly flat when taken off the stretcher. If the design is wobbly, it will mean that the beads were not carefully picked. It takes practice and patience to do nice, even beadwork, and there is nothing more gratifying than to be able to say, "I made it."

Gaps should not be left between the beads when sewing them down. For an even job, it should be sewed between every second or third bead.

PEYOTE BEADWORK

This particular type of beading is put on rattle handles and on quills of feathers in fans used in Peyote ceremonies. It also is used on little rabbit-feet charms, neckerchief slides, horses and other objects made by Pueblo children. Any shaped object can be covered by this method.

Figure 19 shows how this work is done. The beads always are sewed to a cloth or buckskin base, because in irregular objects, the ends must be fastened. In beading round objects such as tubular neckerchief slides, rattle handles, and bases of bonnet feathers, there are no ends, but the beads should rest on some sort of cushion.

A, Figure 19, shows the beginning, but the beads actually should be close together. The drawing is schematic merely to show the threads. B shows how the second string of beads is sewed on. This also is shown in diagram fashion, but in reality the beads are so close together that very little thread is seen as shown in C. This beading, of course, is made with one bead at a time, but beautiful work can

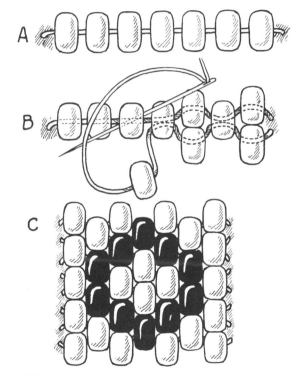

Fig. 19

be done in this manner. Selected beads are a *must* as any irregular beads show up and spoil the effect.

SECTION 2

Upper: Sioux clan of Koshare dancers and their beaded costumes.

Left: Koshare drummers.

Lower left: Koshare dancer in woodland. Beaded dance costume.

Lower right: Koshare dancers know the value of beadwork on their costumes.

Upper left: Looms. On the right loom a pocket comb is used as a spacer.

Upper right: Woodland Sioux bandoleer bag. Appliqued beadwork.

Lower left: Detail of bandoleer bag.

Lower right: Koshare boy and large homemade loom.

Upper left: Ojibwa bandoleer bag (loom beaded).

Upper right: Loom beading applied to medicine bag.

Left: Navajo loom-beaded bag. Design taken from Navajo rug.

Bottom: Wide loom-beaded belt sewed onto heavy harness leather.

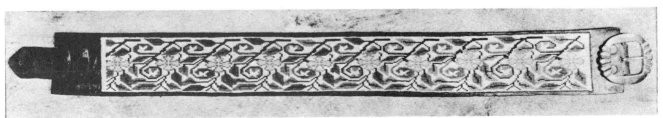

Upper: Belts and bands.

Center: Belt, arm bands, and legging strips.

Lower: Sioux bonnet brow band. Lazy-squaw stitch.

Top: Woodland breechcloths or aprons.

Center: Woodland apron.

Bottom: Appliqué beading. Pair of aprons showing white pencil outlines "A," outline beading "B," and filled-in finished beading.

Top: Breechcloth made by Koshare boy.

Center: Woodland beaded belt. Sewed beadwork.

Bottom: Detail of woodland beaded belt.

Chippewa woman's skirt from Lac du Flambeau. Made of selected beads and beautifully worked.

Woodland men's leggings. A fine example of appliqued beadwork.

Ojibwa beaded bandoleer bag.

Woodland Sioux bandoleer bags.

Left: Top — Woodland Sioux, modern Sioux, and Sioux pipe bags. Bottom — Arapaho, modern Sioux, and Sioux pipe bags.

Center: Western Sioux pipe bag and cuffs. Lazy squaw stitch.

Right: Pipe bag beaded by Koshare boy. Upper of prairie-dog skin.

Bottom: Beaded bags from various western tribes.

Top: Modern beadwork from Arapaho and Cheyenne tribes. Most of these articles were made for tourist trade.

Bottom: Sioux women's leggings and hat-and-head bands.

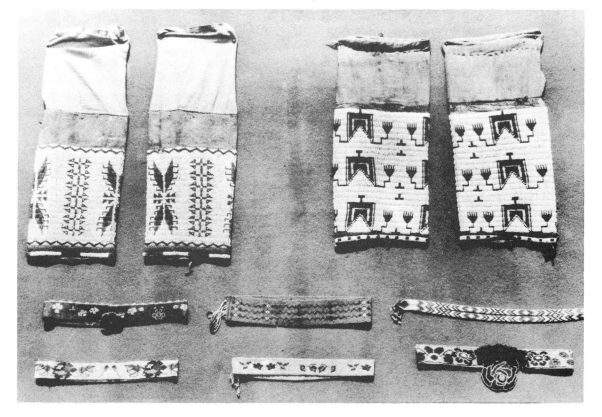

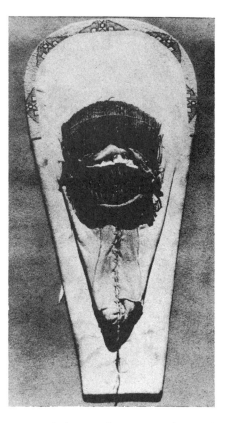

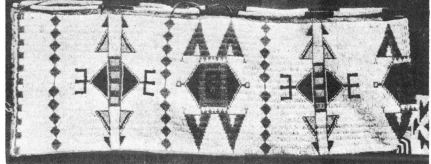

Upper left: Modern Arapaho and Cheyenne small purses.

Upper right: White Ute cradleboard. White buckskin for boys; yellow for girls.

Center: Beaded Blackfoot cradleboard cover.

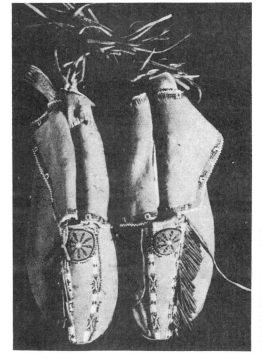

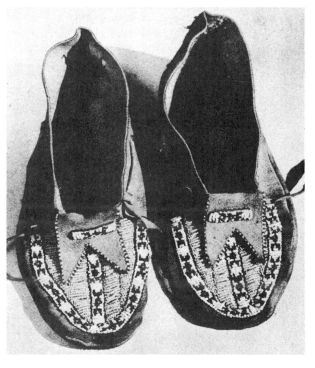

Lower left: Ute moccasins.

Lower right: Moccasins of split cowhide and lazy-squaw beading, made by white boy.

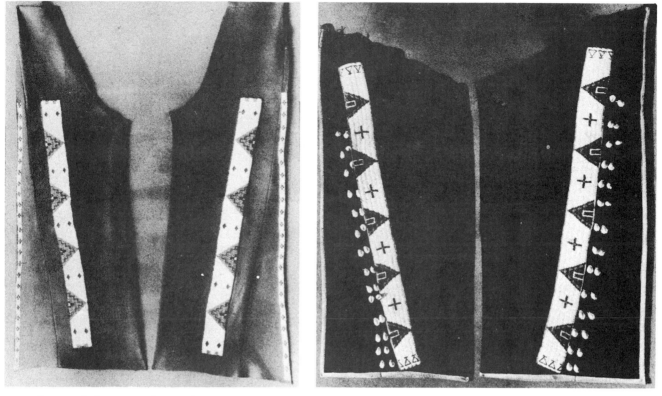

Upper left: Sioux design felt leggings. Made by Buck Burshears.

Upper right: Sioux leggings from Charley Yellowboy. Black blanket cloth.

Lower: Left — Pipe bag; center — quill work and collar, probably Blackfoot; right — roach ornaments.

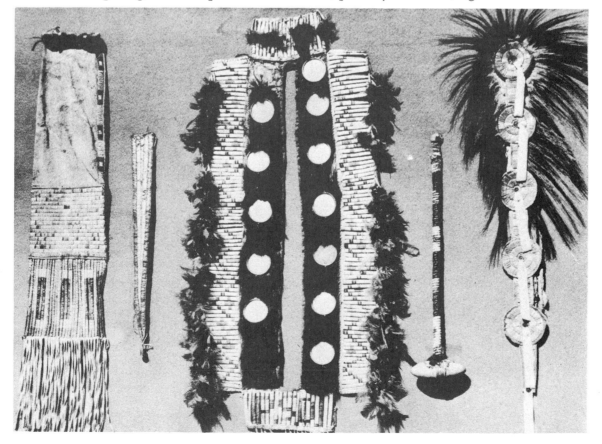

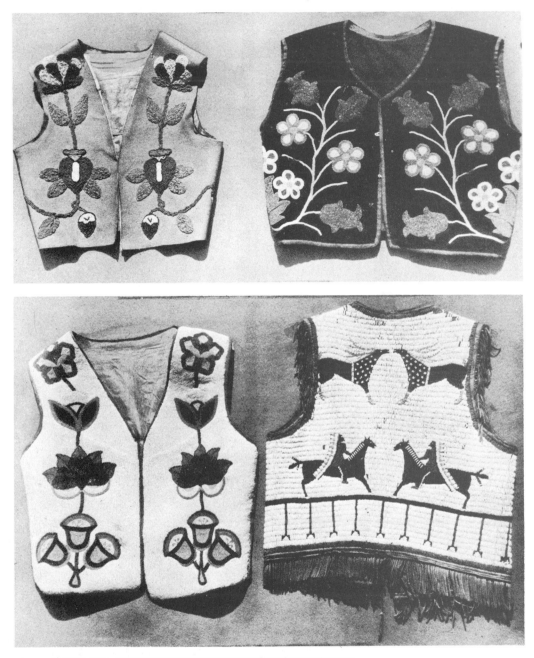

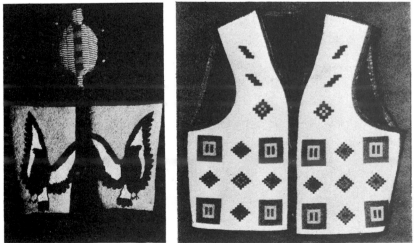

Top: Left—Blackfoot design on orange felt. Made by Koshare boy.
Right — Chippewa vest.

Center: Left — Crow vest made by Minnie Long Nose, 92 years old. Turquoise-blue background.
Right — Cheyenne vest.

Lower left: Beaded turtle charm and pair of cuffs.

Lower right: Beautifully beaded modern Kiowa vest. Applique work with all beading in horizontal lines.

Left: Chippewa woodland yokes from Lac du Flambeau.

Right: Apache and Ute chokers, neckties, and knife sheaths.

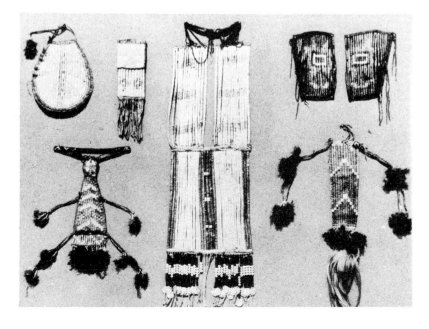

Left: Small bags and necktie.
Center: Quill work — woman's breast plate.

Right: Cuffs and hair ornament, sometimes called Sundance plume.

Top: Beaded cuffs and gauntlet tops.

Bottom: Ute and Bannock gauntlets.

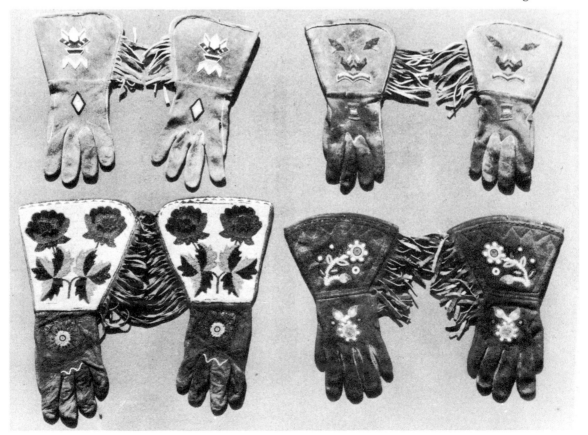

Beaded wall pocket or saddle bag usually hung around tepee.

Sioux beadwork on buckskin covering a valise. Blue background.

Beaded saddlebag. Note that there are about 18 beads on the wide strips and 8 beads on the narrow strips.

SECTION 3

PLATE 1. APACHE AND UTE DESIGNS FOR BELTS

These belt designs are some of the most beautiful examples of beadwork observed while collecting the designs for this book. The upper three designs were taken from belts, and represent half a belt. The middle design was taken from an Apache choker or neckpiece worn by girls in their puberty ceremonials.

The three lower designs came from the Towaoc Ute Reservation, and are good examples of the Ute geometrical designs. The lower design was the decoration on a Ute white buckskin cradleboard. Because the cradleboard was white buckskin meant that it was a boy's, but if it had been yellow or tan, it would have been a girl's.

PLATE 2. SIOUX DESIGNS

This is a collection of Sioux geometrical designs showing various symbols such as the Sioux star, four winds, turtle, rainbow, and the lower piece, the mountain and lake symbols.

PLATE 3. SIOUX DESIGNS

These Sioux designs were found on belts, arm bands, and leg bands.

PLATE 4. SIOUX AND CHEYENNE GEOMETRICAL DESIGNS

These are good designs for arm bands and border decoration, and can be used on cuffs and pocketbooks. Similar designs also have been used by the Utes for hatbands.

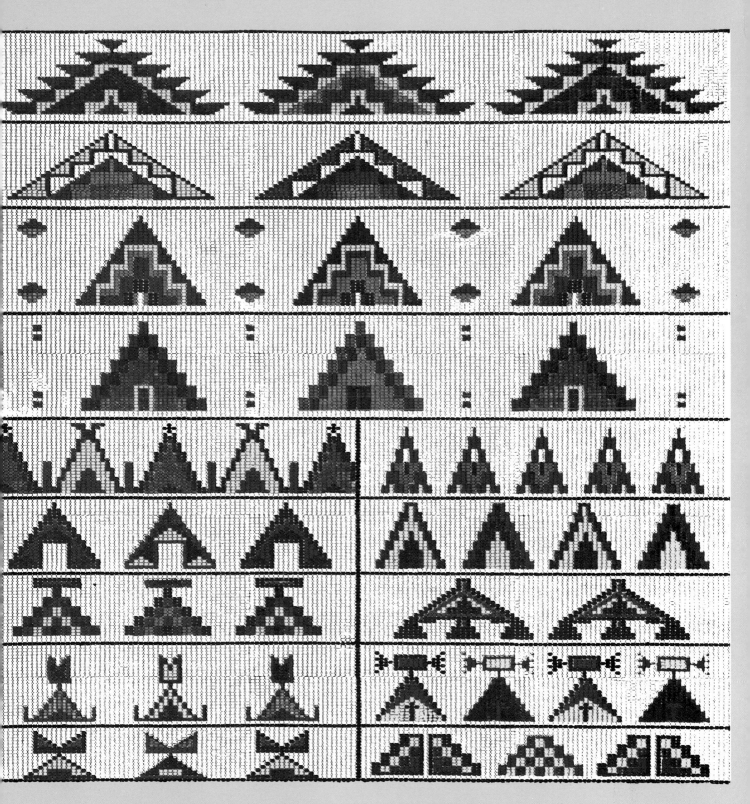

PLATE 5. UTE, SIOUX, AND CHEYENNE DESIGNS

These are the tepee and mountain symbols that come from the Ute, Sioux, and Cheyenne headdress brow bands. It was more or less the style among most tribes to use this type of design as brow bands on headdresses.

These designs with variations can be found in many Indian beaded pieces, as for example, on cuffs, saddlebags, pocketbooks, squaw dresses, hatbands, blanket strips, etc.

PLATE 6. LAKE INDIAN DESIGNS

Lake Indian geometrical and floral abstractions were found on belts and shoulder straps. The floral piece at the top and the grapes second from the bottom show European influence, while the center design gives the impression of a rattlesnake design also found among the Sioux, Utes, Apaches, and others.

PLATE 7. MISCELLANEOUS REDUCED DESIGNS

The designs on this plate have been copied from the other designs previously illustrated. They are repeated here to show that large designs can be easily reduced to meet the needs of the beadworker without losing the motif and beauty of the original design. These are excellent designs for narrow beaded belts for beginners and for border designs.

PLATE 8. UTE FLORAL DESIGNS

The Ute floral designs, taken from belts and hatbands, are the most popular pieces made by the Utes in recent years. They show the different trend of many tribes in recent years to floral designs. These are definitely realistic floral examples with the exception of the fourth design from the top which shows a butterfly symbol. The Utes also have used horse heads, dogs, and other animals in their loomed belts and hatbands.

PLATE 9. OJIBWA AND UTE FLORAL DESIGNS

These are additional floral designs. All are Utes except the first which is Ojibwa floral abstraction. Note the strawberries in one of these hatbands.

PLATE 10.   BLACKFOOT DESIGNS

Blackfoot bag and cradleband designs usually are large with great masses of solid colors. These designs are applicable to pipe bags and large pieces of beadwork. The lower right four-winds symbol is a beautiful example of Blackfoot designs.

PLATE 11. SIOUX PIPE-BAG AND SADDLEBAG
DESIGNS

All of these designs show a similarity of motif, that of the four winds.
The lower right is claimed to have been an altar cloth used in medicine
ceremonies. It is interesting to note the definite cross on the mountain
symbols. It shows a possible Christian influence.

PLATE 12. SHIRT AND ARM STRIPS

The first and second designs at the top to the left are Ogallala Sioux shirt and arm strips, the third is an Apache design, and the rest are Sioux designs.

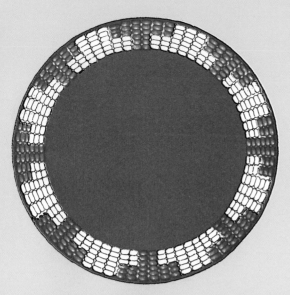

ARAPAHO

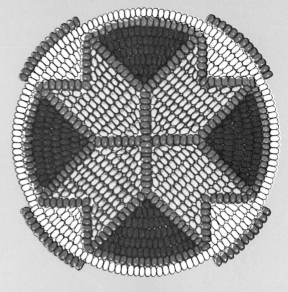

SIOUX

SIOUX

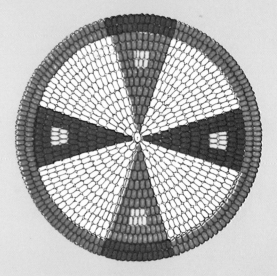

SIOUX

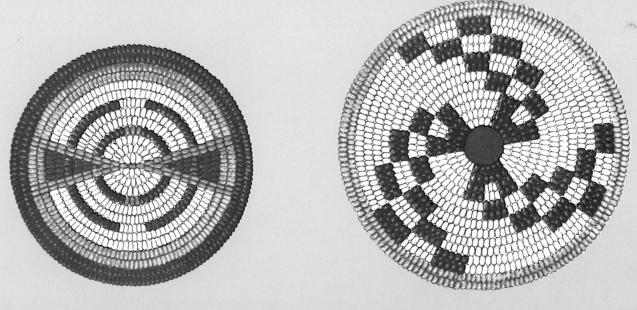

SHOSHONI   *ROSETTES*   **BLACKFOOT**

ZUNI

BLACKFOOT

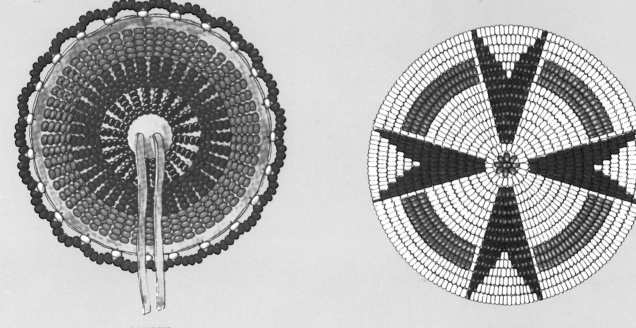

SIOUX

CREE

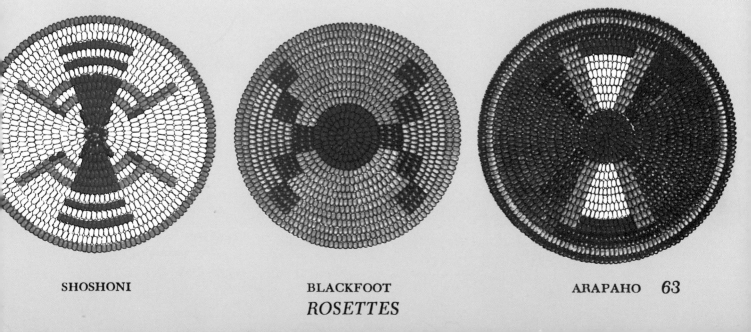

SHOSHONI

BLACKFOOT

ARAPAHO 63

ROSETTES